Sung in a Sensual Style

Rekha Surya

KNOWLEDGE WORLD

KW Publishers Pvt Ltd
New Delhi

ISBN 978-93-83649-26-6

Published in India by Kalpana Shukla

KNOWLEDGE WORLD
KW Publishers Pvt Ltd
4676/21, First Floor, Ansari Road, Daryaganj, New Delhi 110002
Phone: +91 11 23263498/43528107
Email: knowledgeworld@vsnl.net • www.kwpub.com

Printed and Bound in India

2011 FPBA BEST PUBLISHERS AWARD (ENGLISH)

North Indian Light Classical Vocal Music:

Thumri and its Allied Forms

Dedicated to

Begum Akhtar

Girija Devi

with gratitude

Photo courtesy: Sangeet Natak Akademi

Contents

Introduction

Thumri bridges the gap between classical and mainstream music. Its stress on poetry rather than music separates it from the classical realm, while its treatment of classical music separates it from mainstream music. It touches both worlds but is primarily a part of classical music. Its matrix is romance—painful jealousy aroused by a philandering lover, the ache of separation, joyful union or its anticipation.

Musicologists surmise that Thumri's seeds may be traced to 4th century BC when in Vaishali the beautiful and brilliant courtesan Amrapali—reputedly proficient in 64 arts—must surely have sung romantic songs as an art-form.

The role of the courtesan in developing this style has been considerable. Having learnt music under the tutelage of *ustads* and *pandits*, renowned courtesan-singers gave Thumri such stature that it spilled outside the courtesan's domain into the repertoire of male classical stalwarts of the 20th century like Bade Ghulam Ali Khan, Barkat Ali and Abdul Karim Khan.

This genre has a strong feminine presence in poetry laden with unabashed sensuality. Rooted in a sophisticated civilization which drew no line between eroticism and spirituality as in ancient temple sculptures, early Hindu society was emancipated, allowing women to express romantic yearnings. Islam disallowed women to do so. As art mirrors society, only a male voice is heard in Ghazal. Hindu society became puritanical when historically impacted by the Islamic veil and later by Victorian morality. Retaining British prudery, newly independent India denied entry into All India Radio premises to any *baiji* (courtesan-singer) unable to produce a marriage certificate, as stated in All India Radio's archives.

In a seminar on Thumri in 1984, Bade Ghulam Ali Khan's son said "Thumri prospered under *tawaaif*-s (courtesans) but later was considered so unrespectable that classical musicians recoiled from it like vegetarians from non-vegetarian food." Thumri rose above its subaltern status through exponents like Siddheshwari Devi and Begum Akhtar. Post-modern India had Menaka Bai's daughter Shobha Gurtu and Girija Devi as foremost Thumri singers. It is now customary for most Khayal recitals to conclude with Thumri.

North Indian light classical vocal music has three stylistically inter-related segments—Thumri and its nexus of Dadra, Hori, Chaiti, Kajri, Jhoola, Sawan; Ghazal sung traditionally as Thumri's offspring; mystical poetry of the *bhakti-shringar* tradition, in which spiritual and romantic interpretations overlap.

Song-translations are included in these pages for illustrative purposes. Thematically relevant couplets and stanzas added to song-texts are in italics.

Preface

I was eleven years old when I first attended a Khayal concert in my hometown Lucknow, after which I wanted to learn classical music.

Some years later, I met Begum Akhtar who also lived in Lucknow. A common family friend had arranged a meeting in her home, where I was graciously received but my request to learn from her was flatly refused. She said that *talkh tajurben shagirdon key saath* (bitter experiences with students) had made her decide to stop teaching. Just as I was about to leave, she told me to sing something for her. I sang one of her recorded *ghazals* and she dramatically said *sirf isliye ke ye aawaaz zaaya na jaaye, mein tumhe sikhaongi* (I'll teach you just so this voice doesn't go waste) *toh kal subha tum dus baje aajana* (so come tomorrow at 10 am).

The next day I began learning from her. Whenever my father fetched me from her house she would tell him, "You must allow this girl to sing on stage". After morning classes she often told me to stay for lunch. In the afternoons we lay chatting on her bed while she stoked the embers of her past.

She told me that sin meant *kisi ka dil dukhaana* (hurting someone's feelings) and added *mainey kabhi kisi ka bura nahin chaaha hai* (I have never wished anyone ill). She believed that *aik achchey fankaar hone ke liye aik achcha insaan hona zaroori hai* (to be a good artist it is necessary to be a good person). Once when I had taken a gift for her she immediately telephoned my home to say that though not from her womb I was her child so there was no need for presents. She kept out-of-season fruit for me and began taking me with her for concerts. In Calcutta I saw a man prostrate himself at her feet in adulation. Ammi, as she was called by almost everyone who knew her, died much too soon.

A couple of years later, Girija Devi came to Lucknow to perform. I was invited to hear her sing, accompanied by Gudai Maharaj on Tabla, at the home where she was staying. The host told her that my *taleem* under Begum Akhtar had been cut short. She asked about my plans to continue learning music, offered to teach me and told me to accompany her back to Benares after a few days. So I took the train with her to Benares, where I attended a memorable Chaiti concert held soon after Holi—upon entering a *maidaan* we were served *thandai* in earthen bowls while on an open stage several male singers in white *dhotis* sat cross-legged in a neat semi-circle and soon began to sing *chaiti*-s, improvising in turns.

Benares had electricity shortage, leading to severe self-pity during *riyaaz* while sweat trickled down my back. After lessons I was usually sent with a house member on a rickshaw to drink Benarsi *lassi.* Once Kishan Maharaj came over and invited me to his house where in his *aangan* he proudly showed me the varieties of pigeons he reared, pointing out their identifiable differences. Inside his house he introduced me to portraits of his ancestors—all Tabla-maestros.

I went to Benaras intermittently till Girija Devi accepted the post of Guru at Sangeet Research Academy in Calcutta. I joined SRA for a year, during which it organized a week-long seminar on Thumri—eminent musicologist Thakur Jaidev Singh and others analyzed the genre and excavated its origin. I gleaned facts about Thumri and its allied forms from that seminar and from my gurus, who I have frequently quoted here for the benefit of future practitioners of this genre, while twirling the subject around to view it from all angles for the layperson as well.

A Brief History of North Indian Music

Indian music in its nascent stage was formalized around 1500 BC during the Vedic period, when chanting verses from the Vedas in fixed musical patterns were called Samagan. It attained heights by 4th century BC, extending its influence from China to the Mediterranean region.

About 350 BC, the grammarian Panini mentioned Shruti in his writings. Calculated with mathematical exactitude, *shruti*-s or microtones divide tonal space between notes. The historian Sir W. W. Hunter stated that India's 22 microtones existed before the age of

Panini and reached Europe in 11th century AD via Arabia.

Bharat Muni's Natya Shastra, dated variously between 2nd century BC and 3rd century AD, is a treatise on drama, music and dance. Scientific in spirit, its 9 chapters on music elaborate on *swara*-s (musical notes), *shruti*-s (microtones), 2 *grama*-s (scales) *murchana*-s (scales created by transposition) and *jati*-s (precursor to raga-s).

Drawing from the Natya Shastra, Matanga's Brhatdesi written in the 5th century AD is the earliest reference to Raga. Brhatdesi means "a document on popular music". From the same century, a Panchtantra fable also shows Raga's popularity.

Written in the 13th century, Sarangdeva's Sangeet Ratnakar enumerates 264 *raga*-s and expounds the common theory underlying north and south Indian music.

Music in north India flourished in the 16th century during Akbar's reign. His minister Raja Man Singh of Gwalior keenly patronized

Dhrupad, which was later superseded by Khayal. Beginning as indigenous music, modified by migrant Central Asian musicians, Khayal was further developed by Delhi's mystic-poet-musician Amir Khusro in the 13th century and taken forward by Jaunpur's ruler Sultan Sharqui in the 15th century. Its form was crystallized in the 18th century by Sadarang and Adarang who were court-musicians of Delhi's emperor Mohammad Shah.

When Moghul rule collapsed, Delhi's musicians sought patronage from princely courts where they remained throughout the British period. These courts then intensified their cultivation of music, as in Lucknow, Rampur, Gwalior, Jaipur, Baroda and Indore.

*"After the granting of its charter in 1600, the East India Company sent out ships to India every year with a view to establishing regular commerce. Music played a prominent part in these early missions, with consorts of musicians acting as diplomatic 'extras' to ambassadors, and

lavish keyboard instruments being transported to India as presentation gifts to Mughal rulers. Having been granted the right to trade, the Company set up its first permanent settlement in Surat, and this was followed by the opening of many small stations. In the latter part of the 17th century, the larger stations began to develop a musical life almost multi-cultural in character, which made prominent use of Indian dancers and musicians. On public occasions, such as the annual parade to mark the birthday of the sovereign, it was the practice to hire a full 'naubat'.

The early 18th century saw the focus of the Company's activity shift steadily away from Surat and Bombay across to Bengal where Calcutta, effectively an English urban creation on Indian soil, was founded.

The background to the intense fashion for Indian songs and instruments that swept through Anglo-Indian society in the 1780s lies in the expansion of the East India Company's interests into the central and northern provinces of India. It is noteworthy that although Indian tunes were performed and published in Calcutta, they were rarely collected there. Calcutta was perceived as what it was—an English creation. To experience truly 'authentic' Indian culture, it was widely recognized that a journey inland would be necessary, and an ideal location existed—the kingdom of Oudh. A voyage of two or three months up the Ganges, at the leisurely tourist rate of progress, would bring the visitor to the historic cities of Benares and Lucknow, the Company's most important inland stations. The strategic importance of the kingdom grew even as the Mughal Empire waned. Asaf-ud-Daullah came to be regarded by the English as a libertine with no aptitude for serious governance. Company officials thus began to assume a much more active role in ordering the affairs of state. The maintenance of a public show of good relations was now regarded as a top priority, and social intercourse with the Indian nabob and his chief ministers became an important symbol of policy.

Coincidentally with its rise in importance in the strategic affairs of the Company, Lucknow was beginning to emerge as one of the most vigorous musical centres in India. The cause of this was the movement of musicians away from the once dominant centres of Mughal power. Following the death of Mohammed Shah in 1748, there was an exodus of musicians out of Delhi to Oudh, first to Faizabad and then to Lucknow, where the nawabs enjoyed a growing reputation as patrons of culture."

In the 19th century the Naghmat-e-Asafi, written by Patna's nobleman Mohammad Reza, dismissed the earlier Raga-Ragini-Putra classification of music—principal *raga*-s with secondary *raga*-s as wives and derivative *raga*-s as children. Instead, it grouped *raga*-s with commonality under 10 parent scales. Propagated as Thata by Maharashtra's Pandit Bhatkhande in the 20th century, these 10 scales are considered fundamental to north Indian classical music.

As the cry of an animal or bird tends to always have the same pitch, music lore labeled Shadja (*sa*) peacock, Rishabh (*re*) cow's call to her calf, Gandhar (*ga*) goat's bleat, Madhyam (*ma*) heron, Pancham (*pa*) nightingale, Dhaivata (*dha*) horse's neigh and Nishad (*ni*) elephant's trumpeting.

References:
The Music of India by H. A. Popley
Hindustani Music by G. H. Ranade
Indian Music by Chaitanya Deva
Fundamentals of Raga and Tala by Nikhil Ghosh
Music of the Raj by Ian Woodfield

The Concept of Raga and Tala

Western classical musicians interpret compositions while Indian classical musicians improvise upon compositions. The Western device of harmony weaves together multiple strands of music. Indian classical music constructs a single melody. Western rhythm is linear. Indian rhythm is cyclic, with a precise beginning in every time-cycle to gauge duration. The Western method of teaching and learning music employs written notation, whereas Indian music is taught and learnt in an oral tradition.

Classical music differs in aesthetics even within India. Having common roots entrenched in ancient scriptures, the Raga system of music grew separately in north and south India.

In the vast Raga galaxy, each *raga* is a melody with a prescribed structure. It can have all 7 notes (*sampoorna*) or 6 notes (*shadav*) or 5 notes (*aurav*). It has a specific scale of ascent (*aaroh*) which may or may not resemble its scale of descent (*avroh*). It stresses a predominant note (*vadi*) and a subservient note (*samvadi*). It has a distinctive gait (*chalan*) and is recognizable by a recurrent musical phrase (*pakad*). It may linger on notes in the lower or higher register and accordingly is termed *purvanga* or *uttarang*. This modal identity is the basis for the song-composition, which portrays a *raga*'s characteristics and serves as a spring-board for improvisation. Termed *bandish* which literally means "bound", the song-composition consists of 2 parts—the *sthayi* uses notes of the lower and middle octave (*saptak)*; the *antara* uses notes in the upper register.

The Sanskrit word *raga* means "the effect of colouring people's hearts". The mood of a *raga* entails the rigid time theory which dictates when it should be sung, linking it with a particular time of day or night and sometimes with a season.

Raga is harnessed by the rhythmic cycles of Tala played on Tabla.

Tala is a framework of fixed beats measuring a unit of time. Its clockwise movement reflects Kaalchakra or the wheel of time. Each variety of Tala emphasizes the first beat of a time-cycle, a moment of arrival and departure termed *sam*, an abbreviation of *samadhi* or the spiritual state of merging with Divinity. The tempo or Laya used in Taal can be *drut* (fast), *madhya* (medium) or *vilambit* (slow).

In the word *tala*, "ta" represents "tandav" or dancing Shiva's masculine divine energy; "la" represents "lasya" or Parvati's feminine divine energy. When both these energies interact, the loud and soft beats acquire the gait of a *tala*.

Tala has another metaphysical dimension—the empty, gentle portion termed *khaali* connotes the silence of divinity; the full, aggressive portion termed *bhari* connotes loud worldliness. Both portions move through the realms of duality, the *sam* turning the flow of time into a flow of timelessness.

Thumri's Characteristics

Thumri is Abhinayatmak Sangeet or music that enacts emotions. During my first lesson with Begum Akhtar, she showed me how to sing a word within three notes in as many different ways as possible, while expressing the emotional content of the word. This was a rudimentary lesson in Bol-banaana, the idiom on which Thumri's format rests. Melodic variations of a word or phrase display a singer's range of imagination and creativity. Once while chatting about music during a lesson, Begum Akhtar marveled at an erstwhile Thumri singer, "Usually, in ten variations two or three are praiseworthy but her every variation was remarkable—each variation led to another of equal brilliance." Bol-banaana defines Thumri.

When deconstructed, Bol-banaana has components of *khatka, murki, kan* (embellishments) and *meend* (gliding over *shruti*-s) with elements of *pukaar* (which literally means to call out), *dard* (expressing anguish), *uchcharan* (its diction is more emphatic than in Khayal) and *kahan* (speech-intonation).

Thumri concludes with Tabla's speed-driven Laggi. Its rhythmic density of doubled or quadrupled tempo maintains the original pulse, allowing the singer to improvise without changing pace. Bol-banaana within Laggi's intricate grammar is called Takraar in Lucknow Gharana. Laggi ends with a *tihai*—a pattern repeated thrice in succession ending on the *sam*. The conventional practice is to return briefly to the opening *vilambit laya*, for closure. The modern trend is to end in a climax of Laggi.

The compositions are set to the *tala*-s Deepchandi, Chachar, Jat, Teental, Sitarkhani, Addha and Punjabi Theka, mainly in the *raga*-s Bhairavi, Khamaj, Tilang, Des, Manjh-Khamaj, Tilak Kamod, Kafi, Pilu, Jogia, Jhinjhoti, Gara and Pahari.

Thumri stems from Shringar Rasa or romantic love. The Natya Shastra listed Shringar Rasa as one of the primary 8 universal emotions which govern human experience. Glimpsed as the many facets of love, *rasa*-s like Karuna (compassion), Adbhut (wonder), Raudra (anger) and Hasya (laughter) can be drawn into the folds of Shringar Rasa.

The Natya Shastra omits Bhakti. Around the 9th century, Kashmir's Abhinava Gupta added Bhakti to the existing 8 *rasa*-s. Bhakti when entwined with Shringara becomes *madhur bhakti*, an ancient Hindu concept which stretches the emotional repertoire of Thumri beyond physical love, enchantment, longing, separation, passion.

Thumri's *gaayki* or musical aspect addresses *rasa* or universal emotion. Thumri's *sahitya* or literary aspect addresses *bhav* or subjective emotion.

This genre emerged from the region of Uttar Pradesh though its audience is not limited to that area. *Gayaki* can be enjoyed anywhere, like Italian opera. I once asked Begum Akhtar where she most enjoyed singing. I expected her reply to be "Pakistan" or "Hyderabad" because of Urdu-speaking audiences. She answered unhesitatingly, "Poona—*vahan har bol pe daad milti hai* (each improvised phrase is lauded)", as the Maharashtrian love for music demolishes language barriers.

Maharashtra and Bengal have adopted Thumri, using lyrics in the regional language. Maharashtra is influenced by the local flavour of Natyasangeet and Bengal by Punjab-*ang* Thumri.

Improvisation

The creative act is subliminal, coming from sources of which the individual is unaware. *Taleem* (training) of long ago suddenly reappears during *riyaaz* (practice) and moulds *upaj* (improvisation). *Riyaaz* is a route to continuous refinement, a monastic submission to craft, a well of ideas. It is as much a thinking process as it is a physical quest for perfection. This steadily growing intimacy between music and a musician unfolds the latent potential contained in a melody. Seemingly spontaneous phrases in a performance sprout from seeds sown in one's music room, where instinct gains muscle while exploring all possibilities of a melody. Most phrases are re-invented on stage, where musicians rely on pre-determined structures which accommodate phrases steered by impulse. Begum Akhtar once told me, "No one is born a singer—you become one. Nothing is as easy or as difficult as singing."

Peeling away externals, improvisation during internal *maansik riyaaz* includes composing tunes, which can happen while walking or lying in bed. A tune enters my mind while mulling over lyrics, sometimes instantly upon reading powerful poetry. Then I transfer it to the physical world through my harmonium, an instrument that Begum Akhtar had said would help while composing. She taught me basic finger-placement and I learnt to play by replicating whatever I sang.

Differences, Commonalities between Thumri and Khayal

Just as Khayal came into existence by rebelling against the austerity of Dhrupad, Thumri resisted Khayal's constraints of Raga discipline. Being *shabd-pradhan* (word-oriented), Thumri freed itself from the tenets of Raga to unleash emotion in lyrics.

Khayal is tethered tightly to the stringent principles of Raga. By obeying a raga's dictates,

Khayal projects order. Thumri juxtaposes order with disorder by making a form and then breaking it—a method of chaos within order. Thumri permits Raga-deviations by judiciously allowing forbidden notes or meandering into other *raga*-s, returning seamlessly to the predominant raga as gently as tree-leaves fall on grass. Girija Devi uses an analogy for this strict versus lenient adherence to Raga: "Khayal singers sow wheat and reap wheat, whereas Thumri singers sow wheat but reap wheat, millet, barley."

The gradual ascent from note to note, termed Badhat, highlights each note in Khayal. Badhat in Thumri conveys emotions lurking beneath a word or phrase, while ascending notes.

Taan is an integral part of Khayal. Taan's vigour is unsuited to the romantic nature of Thumri and its variants, which occasionally exhibit *sapaat* (straight) or intricate Tappa-style *taan*-s.

Raga paints Khayal and Thumri with different strokes—Khayal is like an abstract painting and

Thumri like a figurative one.

In both Khayal and Thumri, the song or *bandish* delineates a *raga*'s peculiarities and is used as a base. The most important part of the *bandish* is the *mukhda*—a part of the first line concluding on the *sam*. Literally meaning 'face', *mukhda* is a leitmotif which Khayal and Thumri singers repeatedly use as a point of reference. Both Khayal and Thumri have *gharana*-s.

Thumri's Gharanas

The two basic styles of rendering Thumri emanate from Purab (eastern Uttar Pradesh) and Punjab. The Purab style has sub-divisions which encompass Benares, Lucknow and Gaya—each of these cities has its own *gharana*.

Girija Devi says that *suron ka asar*—the effect of stark notes—distinguishes Benares Gharana. The lyrics accentuate absence, memory and longing, encapsulated in the term *birah* which means separation. Benares Gharana's repertoire includes Tappa, said to be a classicized version of the songs of camel-drivers. Composed in Thumri *raga*-s, Tappa uses profusely decorative *taan*-s woven into the song's text.

In Benares and Gaya, the region's folk songs Chaiti and Kajri were classicized to join the ranks of Thumri, unifying rural and urban cultures by suffusing folk poetry with Raga. The Gaya school accepts a *vilambit* (slow) Kaherwa Taal of simple 8 beats instead of the more complex Thumri *taal*-s.

Lucknow Gharana focuses on Thumri, Dadra and Ghazal. Its repertoire includes Hori, Kajri, Jhoola and Sawan but excludes Tappa and Khayal. Lucknow Gharana embraces Urdu poetry, infusing *nazaakat* (delicacy) and *nafaasat* (refinement) into this voluptuous genre. Begum Akhtar told me to always follow a *thumri* with a *ghazal* and then sing a *dadra*, to break the monotony of *bhasa* (language). She also said that the contrast of language sparkles when suitable Urdu couplets are attached to *dadra*-s.

Dadra

In mock anger, Krishna teasingly twists Radha's arm while she pleads with him to let go:

Listen to me my love, I beg you and touch your feet—
Krishna, stop twisting my arm!

A relevant Urdu couplet:
I beg you, fall at your feet, humbly request you—
Even then if you don't listen what can one do?

Dadra

My love has come home—
I've put *kohl* in my eyes, flowers in my hair.
After many days my love has come home—
We laugh and embrace.

Fish shimmer in water, like swords glinting on a battlefield—
The full moon gleams on lovers like my bindi glitters in bed.

(Hindi couplet)

My goals now seem easy as the wind has changed direction—

With your hand holding mine, the road ahead has got lit.

(Urdu couplet)

Lucknow Gharana attracted Bade Ghulam Ali Khan, who then clothed Thumri's literary texts with Punjab's ornate melodic style. Punjab's Thumri uses complex note-combinations and *phirat* (swift movement of notes). Purab's Thumri uses *behlava* (to cajole) and *pukaar* (to call out) in Bol-banaana. Pondering the difference between both styles, Girija Devi once told me that emotional Purab Thumri has the simplicity of a village-belle whereas flamboyant Punjab Thumri has the glamour of a city-woman.

The Allied forms of Thumri

Faster-paced than Thumri, Dadra gets its name from the word *dadur* meaning frog, as its rhythmic movement resembles frog-leaps. Dadra's musical variations should be tightly plaited with the rhythm, maintaining the rhythmic lilt. The crisp Bol-banaana in Dadra, of a phrase rather than a word, is more challenging than the leisurely, unconstrained, spacious Bol-banaana in Thumri, generally of a word rather than a phrase.

Dadra

Radha is tortured by Krishna's infidelity:

What spell have you cast Krishna,
To push me off the edge of sanity?

In that lane you come and go,
Making up lame excuses to me.

You laugh and chat with another,
Burning me who is already burnt.

The almost obsolete social order of joint families is central to many light classical texts. Such lyrics are anachronistic and socially irrelevant today but are valued for antiquity.

Dadra

How to tip-toe with my tinkling anklets?

My fanciful love has decorated the bed,
Only after that, he's asked me to come.

Such a noise my wretched anklets make—
My sister-in-law's awake!

My heart thuds though it isn't mine,
Whenever my anklets tinkle.
I'm very young and I might be heard,
Whenever my anklets tinkle.
(Stanza by Nawab Wajid Ali Shah of Lucknow.)

Dadra

A wistful nayika describes her disappointment to her sister-in-law:

I felt sleepy so fell asleep, sister-in-law—
My love came and went from my door!

I picked flowers and decorated my bed,
I adorned myself then gazed at the lane…
Waiting, I fell asleep and awoke to find—
My love came and went from my door!

Associated with the Indian calendar, the seasonal varieties of Thumri and Dadra are Jhoola, Kajri, Sawan, Hori and Chaiti.

Jhoola, which literally means "swing", captures the scent of rain-drenched earth after sweltering heat, when village-girls joyfully swing on wooden planks tied with ropes to trees. Jhoola conveys the swaying movement of a swing in its text and musical treatment. Kajri-texts usually bemoan separation from one's beloved during the rainy season. Kajri and Jhoola are sung Dadra-style. Sawan, also monsoon-related, is sung Thumri-style.

Hori and Chaiti are sung as either Thumri or Dadra. Hori-texts spring from the frolicsome Holi festival.

Chaiti—sung during the month of Chait following Holi when Rama's birth is celebrated as Ramnaumi—has the mandatory phrase "ho Rama". This salutation distinguishes Chaiti from other light classical forms.

Chaiti

In the month of Chait the nightingale sings
in my courtyard, ho Rama!

'Kuhuk-kuhuk' the black nightingale sings,
Wrenching pain from my heart, ho Rama!

When I remember my love's embrace,
My eyes well up with tears, ho Rama!

Kajri

Dark clouds swirl in the skies while
My bed is empty without Krishna!

Tears pour like rain as I pine for him—
What can I do with my heavy heart?
Lightning flashes, thunder and rain—
My bed is empty without Krishna!

A relevant verse by Josh Malihabadi:

Raindrops pierce my heart,

Burning me in your absence,
Stinging my whole being, as
They slash this way and that.

Kajri

I'm wet in the rain my love,
Please come and shelter me!

My blouse is soaking wet
And it makes me feel shy,
My female form is visible—
I beg you cover me, hide me!

Jhoola

My heart sways along with the swing,
Since my Krishna sits on it beside me.

This swing is unique and so precious,
Since my Krishna sits on it beside me.

Dancing peacocks amid lush foliage
With a delicate drizzle creates magic!

Jhoola

The heavy, dark clouds hang low—
Swinging on the swing is Krishna.

On the *kadamba* tree is a swing with silken ropes—
Swinging on the swing is Krishna.

Sway! Sway! Sway! My girlfriends push with gusto—
Swinging on the swing is Krishna.

Hori

Don't use force on me Krishna, while we play Holi!

Oh look! Krishna just won't not let go of my arms and
Holds me tight, so the seams of my blouse have burst!

The colourful Holi powders fly around as a hazy cloud,
In which I take cover, quietly creep home, slinking away!

Hori

Holi has come, but my love has not—
Now who wants to play with colour!

My girlfriends play with gay abandon
With their veils and their blouses wet.
Standing alone, apart from the others,
Ready with colours, I stare at the lane.......

Holi has come, but my love has not—
Now who wants to play with colour!

The gender of the first person in these texts is always feminine and in Ghazal is always masculine.

Thumri's Relationship with Ghazal

Recited and also sung by Urdu poets in *mushaira*-s, Ghazal was adopted by musicians who gave its burgeoning popularity a distinct musical identity termed *ghazal-gayaki*—an offspring of Thumri. In his dissertation during the 1984 Thumri Seminar conducted by Sangeet Research Academy, the eminent musicologist Thakur Jaidev Singh included Ghazal, illustrated with recordings.

Trained to emote and pour passion into

a text, Thumri singers render Ghazal aptly, though familiarity with Urdu poetry is a requisite and restraint in Bol-banaana is necessary. If a couplet is swamped with excessive musical treatment, the poetic thread between the two lines gets lost, weakening their cohesion. Begum Akhtar explained the relationship between the literary and musical aspects of Ghazal by telling me "Ghazal's poetry and its musical presentation are like a painting and its frame—a painting should be decorated, not dwarfed, by its frame just as the poetry in Ghazal should be enhanced, not eclipsed, by its music."

The singer becomes the song by closely following the poetry and identifying with a poet's utterance.

Ghalib

Is it my sorrow that unsettles you? Alas!
What became of your indifference? Alas!

What if you vowed lifelong love?
Life itself is most uncertain. Alas!

To shyly hide beneath dust and earth
Is the ultimate veil of modesty. Alas!

The swordsman lacks practise
So can't pierce my heart. Alas!

Untouched by madness, ardour
Remains unripe within me. Alas!

Ghazal's Literary Aspect

Ghazal as a literary form is 800 years old. Its origins are traced to pre-Islamic Arabia. Arriving in India from Persia, it adapted to the Indian ethos by finding its groove in Urdu—a language having a medley of Hindi, Turkish, Persian and Arabic words with an Indic base.

Originally confined to the subject of love, Ghazal has a plaintive tone ascribed to romantic anguish. Later, major poets pushed back its boundaries to extend its parameters beyond romance.

The layperson often confuses Nazm—termed Geet when sung—with Ghazal. Nazm has one single train of thought running through a poem. Its thematic continuity has natural progression, whereas Ghazal is fragmented by discrete couplets that evoke varying sentiments. These unlinked couplets are unified by inflexible technical rules. Within a chosen meter, the opening couplet (*matla*) establishes a scheme of rhyme (*qaafia*) and refrain (*radeef*), the rhyme preceding the refrain in both lines. This scheme recurs in the second line of each succeeding couplet. These structural constraints are a sharp contrast to Ghazal's thematic freedom, as each couplet has independent thought-content. A couplet compresses a complete poem into just two lines, resonating Japanese Haiku minimalism.

Jigar Moradabadi

One word of love contains just a common story—
Unspoken it is pure but if spoken, it gets sullied.

Love isn't easy so understand this—
It is a river of fire to swim across.

Love and pain are two sides of a picture—
One side's concealed, the other revealed.

There are unshed tears in my eyes Jigar, which when
Strung together are pearls but left unstrung are beads.

Majaz Lucknowi

Time makes you forget or just vaguely remember—
Even searing moments fade from memory's edge!

A rich imagination conjures many images
But can no longer recall that beloved face!

Beauty no longer moves me nor blooms the bud in my heart—

Springtime is lush and abundant but I am unable to savour it.

My loyalty's matched by your cruelty—
A dagger near my vein lies forgotten.

Altaf Hussain Hali

My quest is to find supreme perfection—
Now let us see where my gaze will rest!

The one whom I adore is singularly special—
Many surpass her yet for her alone I yearn!

My prayer for this bond to break isn't answered—
What the heart doesn't really want isn't granted!

Hali, you set out too late for music and wine—
You come at dawn, where were you all night?

Mir Taqi Mir

Love just sprouted and you weep?
What lies ahead is yet to be seen!

This soil of love doesn't yield much—
Why sow seeds of desire in arid land?

The caravan has a morning clarion-call—
"Shake off your sloth for we move on!"

Time is as precious as Yusuf's piety—
Then why let it slip away wastefully?

Thumri and its Ilk Viewed from a Feminist Perspective

The protagonist as a *nayika* (heroine) with the first person in feminine gender has been a tradition perpetuated by many male poets.

Kabir

In my maiden-home, I stained my veil.

The dyer with colours can't set it right,
Nor can any washerman make it bright.

Kabir advises "All else is in vain—
Only love can remove the stain."

Patriarchal dominance and gender inequality are highlighted in this heart-rending Babul (sung when a bride leaves her parental home):

Amir Khusro

Why did you marry me off into a distant land,
beloved father?

To my brothers you've given a palace or two,
But to me what? You've only given me away.

I'm only an innocent bird in your courtyard,
Where I pecked at some seeds and flew away.

I'm just a cow tied to a peg in your courtyard,
And I've to go wherever your stick directs me.

The lyrics of this *dadra* reveal societal attitudes with the stigma attached to women discarded by men:

Keep my dignity or don't, do as you wish.

Our love lasted ten days
And branded me for life.

The *antara* in this *dadra* displays the social vulnerability of women:

This beggar begs for alms of love,
So keep my dignity intact, beloved.

This *chaiti* about a child-bride exposes the social reality of its times:

I was awoken, oh Rama, at dawn.

I was twelve years old when
My husband asked for me.

Harboring bourgeois notions of respectability, one still encounters prejudices of a patriarchal mindset that thinks female singers of romantic poetry merely pander to the male gaze. Uncertain about how I was perceived as a woman-singer in my younger days, I abandoned some career opportunities.

Female practitioners of this art-form are subjected to male scrutiny. Even after Girija Devi attained fame, a male critic's review claimed her success lay in her smiles and physical charm on stage. A media man spoke condescendingly of Begum Akhtar as a great performer but not a great singer. Time is the final judge, as her albums continue to sell more than 30 years after her death.

Begum Akhtar and Girija Devi as Mentors

Begum Akhtar respected tradition without being orthodox. Being eclectic, she once told me, "Listen keenly to all sorts of music. Absorb elements from any source to incorporate into your music. Pick up music from everywhere."

Girija Devi is a staunch Benares Gharana follower as was also Siddheshwari Devi, despite their entirely dissimilar musical approach. Ultimately, individual temperament and vision shape a musical style.

Begum Akhtar approved of Benares Gharana's use of Tappa as initial training for vocal agility and wistfully said she wished I could learn Tappa for *tayyari* (virtuosity). My *taleem* under Girija Devi began with Tappa.

Begum Akhtar believed strongly that *kharaj* (morning practice in the lower octave) sustains vocal steadiness and purity of notes, saying that in her later years she could sing unwaveringly only because she had practiced *kharaj* throughout childhood. Girija Devi did not favour *kharaj* but both gave importance to *palta*-s (vocal exercises).

Their pedagogy transgressed the technicalities of music. Girija Devi once told me "Exposing oneself to other art-forms, like dance, literature and painting, sharpens one's aesthetic sensibilities."

During an initial lesson with Begum Akhtar, she told me to repeat just one *khatka* (an embellishment of a note and a half) innumerable times, saying that her entire *gayaki* was based on the *khatka* technique. Told to continuously repeat it, I did so while she got up and did some household chores, calling out every now and again to correct it from another room.

One of the reasons for her iconic stature rests on this observation while I was on stage with her:

*"She kept her listeners alive to the poetry by keeping them constantly expectant for the *qaafiya*, the 'punch' word which completes the poet's idea in every couplet. She would musically play around with the words prior to it, building anticipation, and then pause for a split second. Her fingers on the harmonium would freeze for a tense moment. Then the *qaafiya* consummated the sense of drama."

*Sangeet Natak Akademi publication: "The Living Legend Becomes a Legend" by Rekha Surya.

The Inclusion of Sufi Poetry in Light Classical Music

Indian prose established itself as late as the 19th century, whereas the long history of Indian poetry has a grip over national psyche. Some saints articulated their thoughts through verse. Many of these verses have verbally traversed centuries and are heard in everyday parlance, particularly those of Kabir.

In the subcontinent, Sufi verses were originally sung as Qawwali, a genre which arose from the influence of Keertan—Hindu devotional group-singing accompanied by brisk rhythm. Qawwali was originally sung in *dargahs* (enshrined tombs of Sufi saints) where its rhythm, music and poetry sometimes induce a *haal* (spiritual trance) in listeners. Its content is more significant than its form, as the poetry outweighs the music sheathing it. This poetry inspired other musical genres to adopt and adapt it to their own styles, making contemporary Sufi music diverse. Wanting to neither follow a popular trend nor resist it, I sing Sufi poetry because its syncretic lyrics project India's secular culture or *Ganga Jamuni tehzeeb* which seeks unity—not uniformity—of fellow-beings. Religion is a divisive factor in societies, whereas Sufism represents mysticism—the core of all belief systems—which connects separate paths.

As an abstract philosophy of sages which later translated into mythology to become tangible for the common man, Hinduism in its primary form addresses the intellectual. The religious laws in Islam address a collective community. Such differences are transcended by the wider significance of Sufism, although Sufism itself is divided into formal sects within Islam.

Beheaded for blasphemy for his cries of "Anal Haq" meaning "I am God", the 9th century Sufi Mansoor echoed the Upanishads—dated around 800 BC—which proclaim on behalf of the individual "Aham Brahma asmi" meaning "I am Brahma".

Sufism mirrors the Hindu concept of *atma* seeking union with *Parmatma*, symbolized in mystical poetry by a woman yearning to unite with her beloved. Ancient Hindu temples adorned with erotic sculpture recognize sensuality as a force that surges beyond the body. With smudged divisions, mysticism has no dichotomy between the physical and the metaphysical, no conflict between form and formlessness, no collision between the worlds of romance and spirituality. An individual's inner cleansing enables the individual's unity with cosmic consciousness, like a drop joining an ocean. Veiled by sensuality, songs with undercurrents of mysticism have parallel themes that are romantic and spiritual, like two sides of a coin.

Dadra

(Origin shrouded in antiquity)

A bride dirties her wedding attire in her parental home (the world) so fears being seen by her bridegroom (God). His lifting of her veil symbolizes the ultimate moment of facing God. Her lack of skills-jewels-virtue indicates a tainted mind-body-soul. Her plea for union with her beloved represents the *atma's* urge to merge with *Parmatma* or the Supreme Consciousness:

> My beautiful sari has got all soiled at my parents' home—
> So how now can I show myself at my husband's home?

I have no etiquette, nor jewels, nor virtue—
So when my beloved lifts my bridal veil,
What excuses can I make?

Your ugly mind lacks compassion so
Why preen yourself before a mirror?

(Kabir)

I'll bathe in the Ganga, worship Surya, fast every Sunday;
Ma Ganga! I'll lay on your waters my veil as an offering—
Cleanse me so I'm ready to meet my beloved!

My love gave me the herb of timelessness, unbinding me
From the cycles of life and death, freeing me from fear—
Then firmly I clasped my love's hand to
Become immaculate, merging in union.

(Tulsi of Hathras)

The path to the river-bank is difficult, so how
Do I fill my pail with water from the Jamuna?
I was about to fill water, when
My vessel broke in an embrace. *

(Amir Khusro)

*The smashed vessel signifies the ego's annihilation—losing oneself to find oneself. In this liberated state of surrender to nothingness, Paramatma embraces atma.

Amir Khusro

The 17th century metaphysical poetry of John Donne and Andrew Marvell is sensual yet spiritual like that of Amir Khusro of the 13th century.

This poem's backdrop is the Indian rainy season, when climatic respite encourages romantic yearnings to seek fulfillment. The beloved's homecoming signifies the Lord's return to one's heart:

The nightingale calls out repeatedly,
While the fair one beautifies herself.

(Amir Khusro)

*[1]My friend! Now that my beloved's come home,
This courtyard has become an auspicious place.

Come on, friends! Let's set up a swing—
My love will return in the rainy season.

If in this season my love isn't here—
Let a fire rage and devour the rain!

I stood waiting, wearing
Henna, kohl, vermilion—
Upon seeing my love's beauty
I lost both my mind and body.

No one's come to my house
So I'll go to my love's house.

*The palanquin has come with its carriers—
I'll adorn myself to go to my love's home.

She who spent the rains with her beloved
Is the bride who will spend a nuptial night.

Someone go tell the moon to go away if it wishes,
As my love's presence shines with as much light!

[1]*In mystical poetry the *sakhi* (confidant) alludes to a *guru* or *pir* (spiritual guide).
[2]*Palanquin-carriers taking the bride to her groom imply pallbearers. Mystics celebrate death as marriage with the Maker.

Amir Khusro

Khusro's couplet echoes the Biblical belief
"The meek shall inherit the earth":

The river of love has an opposite current—
Only those who drown in it reach ashore.

Speak to me or don't, listen or don't—
I'll still never ever leave you, my love.

My in-laws may ignore me,
The village may ignore me,
Only you mustn't ignore me—
I'm now under your shelter.

Where's the need for shy modesty,
When my feet are tied to you, love?
Of my own will I'll stay with you—
From your door where can I go?

Amir Khusro-Mirabai

Three centuries apart, Amir Khusro (13th century) and Mirabai (16th century) used similar metaphors—of colour and the garment—in verses which I combine in this song. The song's refrain is Mirabai's plea to Krishna—*"mori rang de chunariya"* meaning "enlighten me!"

Amir Khusro was the first Muslim mystic who perceived Krishna as the embodiment of love and Krishna's music as a beckoning towards awakened consciousness, as in this introductory verse:

Amir Khusro:

The forest's birds are aflutter, maddened
By such magic of The Dark One's flute!
This unique music enchants the trees
So all their branches sway and dance!
Women going to the well stand still and listen—
Enraptured, Khusro, they forget to fill water!

Mirabai:

Krishna beloved, colour my veil!

I'll accept none, not red nor yellow—
Drench my veil with only your tint!

I won't leave until my veil gets dyed—
Even if my life gets spent in waiting!

Amir Khusro:

Khusro, on my wedding night I lay awake with my beloved—
My body merged with his mind to become the same colour.

Amir Khusro:

My veil, dirtier than those of my girlfriends,
Makes everyone snigger at me—
This spring, brighten my veil with colour to
Replace my shame with dignity.

Sufi thought upholds humanism—the essence of every religion—to discover godliness within. It prods one to expand one's capacity for compassion and to develop the ability to withhold judgement of others. Mysticism celebrates love in totality—human and divine. It suggests that when love spreads outwards and becomes impersonal, it entitles the loving to be forever loved. Shades of Sufism brush the poetry of all mystics, like Mirabai of the Bhakti period:

Mirabai

I love so much it hurts.

Atop the scaffold lies my bed—how can I sleep?
Atop the skies lies my love's bed—how to unite?

I roam restlessly to find a cure, but
Only my beloved can heal this pain.

Shabad (Guru Teg Bahadur)

I haven't seen unconditional love.

Everyone's self-seeking,
Be it a relative or friend.

We're all alone in the end—
Strange are nature's laws!

Everyone says "Mine, mine!"
Which only binds the mind.

"Love comes but where does it go?" ask onlookers.
To weep one moment and laugh the next isn't love.
Love doesn't rise and fall from moment to moment.
Talked about by all, yet love is understood by none!
(Kabir)

Rekha Surya

Sins, big or small, are committed by all—
Who's a sinner around here? Don't ask!

Don't pretend to be nicer than you are.
Be fearless and be open about the truth—
Don't make false friendships seem real.

Till when can you hide your flaws by
Making others small so you seem tall?
While sneering count your own faults.

Don't be a callous spectator of injustice.
Speak out against it with courage or else—
Your silence becomes part of the wrong.

Don't trample on feelings, using
Words that wound and torment—
Think before hurtful utterances.

Earth, sky, wind, fire, water—
These five forces are jointly
The might of God reflected
In human beings who then
Should respect one another.

(Rekha Surya)

Dadra

The lyrics of this *dadra* run parallel to Sufi thought:

Come to my doorway, so that
In beholding you I fall in love.

Reward this beggar who begs only for love—
The meeting of glances resolves all conflict!

Love intoxicates when
My glance meets yours.

(Amir Khusro)

All in the heavens and on earth *
Are gazed upon by divine love.

*Refers to the Sufi belief in 'Tauheed' or oneness in an inter-connected cosmos—I am in you and you are in me. Seeing oneself in all living creatures creates a sympathetic world-view. Self-effacement and identifying oneself with the world outside one lead to a higher level of consciousness.

Performances as Novel Experiences

When communism in Russia repressed religion, a folk form of mysticism called Falak emerged in Tajikistan. The term Falak means "connecting the world to the moon and the stars". Kulyab, a hinterland city in Tajikistan, invited India, Iran, Afghanistan and Uzbekistan to participate in its 2006 Falak Festival.

Of Persian descent, Tajiks venerate their classical poets Firdausi and Omar Khayyam whose poetry was sung at the Falak Festival. The audience responded enthusiastically to my singing the poetry of Amir Khusro whom they reverentially call "Khusro Dehlvi". The Festival authorities gifted me exotic Tajik attire which I wore for my concert in Dushambe's Opera House, where the grandeur of the Tsar era peeps from its magnificent ceiling.

Tajiks are economically weak yet deem it fashionable to have almost all their teeth gold-capped even without dental decay. Archaeologists will find a lot of gold buried in Tajikistan. Once on the trade route of caravans travelling between Persia, China and India, this region is said to have spawned the Aryan race.

The Antecedents and Origin of Thumri

Among the four ancient books of knowledge, the Sama Veda—*sama* means melody and *veda* means knowledge—is the fount of Indian music. The Sama Veda's metric chants or Chhand-Prabandh engendered Dhrupad in north India. Dhrupad germinated in temples but later entered palaces where it prevailed gloriously in the 16th century. Its popularity declined with the rise of Khayal, a musical outcome of Indo-Persian synthesis. Some musicologists regard Thumri as an offshoot of Khayal.

Thumri dominated the culturally vibrant court of Nawab Wajid Ali Shah of Oudh (1822-1887). Most musicologists dismiss the notion that this aesthete originated Thumri, saying that the Harvansh Purana dated between 2nd century B. C. and 2nd century A.D. bears testimony to Thumri's incipience, preceding Dhrupad and Khayal.

Some musicologists assert that Thumri evolved from Holi Dhammar and Haveli Sangeet in 16th century Brindavan. Holi Dhammar uses Khamaj, Pilu and Kafi *raga*-s in 14 beats played on Pakhawaj. Thumri uses the same raga-s in 14 beats played on Tabla. Haveli Sangeet ends in 8 beats Kaherwa Taal like Thumri's concluding Laggi. These commonalities suggest kinship.

Thumri's existence is firmly established in 17th century Braj, which at that time was a much larger area. In 19th century Lucknow, an *ustad* (maestro) called Sadiq Ali Khan gave Thumri today's recognized form. It then reached Benares where it blossomed.

Thumri's Association with Kathak

In the etymology of Thumri, the syllable *thum* is derived from *thumak* or walking with a sway of hips. The syllable *ri* implies femininity and is a form of address to a *sakhi* or female confidante. It is also an abbreviation of *rijhana* meaning "to please".

Thumri is of two types. Bol-banao-thumri has languid Bol-banaana. Bandish-ki-thumri resembles Chota Khayal compositions and is also called Bol-baant-thumri, having phrases distributed by rhythm. When sung as accompaniment for Kathak dancers, both types of Thumri are termed Arth-bhav-thumri.

Thumri became associated with Kathak in Oudh's court of Nawab Wajid Ali Shah. Bindadin Maharaj of Kathak's Lucknow Gharana wrote *thumri*-s. His nephew Shambhu Maharaj sang *thumri*-s to depict their content through *bhav-dikhaana* (gestural dance). Begum Akhtar said he unravelled each emotional nuance wrapped around a word or phrase and created visual images couched in connotations which surrounded that word or phrase. She added that had he not been a great Kathak dancer he would have been a great Thumri singer.

Poets of Thumri-texts

Indian classical music travelled on an oral journey across centuries from villages and temples to palaces. Undocumented poets who wrote *thumri*-s, *dadra*-s, *kajri*-s, *jhoola*-s, *hori*-s, *chaiti*-s may have also authored Khayal compositions, which use common dialects—Brij-bhasa, Khari-boli, Purbi and Awadhi.

By attaching their names to *bandishen*, some composers of Bol-banao-thumri were known to be Qadar Piya, Sughar Piya and Rang Piya; specializing in Bandish-ki-thumri were Sanad Piya, Lallan Piya, Chand Piya and Kunwar Shyam. Bade Ghulam Ali Khan wrote *thumri*-s under the pen-name Sabrang.

The last Moghul king Bahadur Shah Zafar, an Urdu poet, wrote *hori*-s in Khari-boli under the pen-name Shokh Rang. Nawab Wajid Ali Shah wrote *thumri*-s under the pseudonyms Akhtar Piya and Ali. His delicately layered *thumri* "Baabul mora naihar chooto jaye" can be interpreted literally as a bride's lament in having to leave her parental home, or was his personal lament in having to leave his kingdom, or is a universal lament in having to leave the world.

Thumri

Father, my home will get left behind...

Four carriers jointly lifted me up
And I set off for my love's land.

The Effect of Modernity on Light Classical Forms

Like riverside tree-leaves fall in a river and become one with it, contemporary ideas seep into the constantly flowing river of art. Traditions in transition mutate—rooted in the past, shaped by the present, reaching out to the future in unbroken continuity.

No artist is greater than an art-form, in which lies the collective contribution of many artists. An artist may set a trend or cater to a current scenario, raising the question "Do artists create audience-tastes or do audience-tastes create artists?"

Khayal's strictures shield its character, though imperceptible changes creep into even rigorous forms. Liberalism in light classical music has led to drastic changes. Ghazal has undergone transformation—plucked out of a Hindustani light classical repertoire, Ghazal is now presented separately, or is grouped with Geet and Bhajan in the category of Sugam Sangeet (light music). To reach mainstream audiences, Ghazal is often diluted to sound like tune-oriented Geet. In sharp contrast, another trend—with the intent to dazzle—inserts into Ghazal *sargam* and *tihai* culled from Khayal, whereas Ghazal traditionally uses covert musicianship rather than overt virtuosity to safeguard its romantic aura. Ghazal has drifted from Thumri's ambit.

A path-breaker like Mehdi Hassan gave Ghazal a new direction. Begum Akhtar admired his genius, although his vision of Ghazal—unlike hers—was Khayal-oriented, showing no affinity with full-throated Thumri.

As societal changes permeate art, local is sometimes global, making fusion music popular. Even so, tall walls have arisen between classical, light classical and mainstream music in an age of specialization. Khayal audiences are attuned to the slow pace used by Thumri but Ghazal audiences are not. So instead of slow-paced Thumri, I sing faster-paced Dadra, Kajri, Jhoola, and Hori as Ghazal audiences accept the classicism of Bol-banaana when the rhythm is sprightly.

Straying from tradition, I present poems of Kabir and Tulsi of Hathras written in the literary form of Ghazal as *ghazal*-s, not *bhajan*-s. Kabir's poetry was compiled in the Bijak about a century after his death by his disciples, some of who propagated his thoughts in chosen forms like Ghazal. Mirabai's thoughts are also represented by her disciples from different regions, as the dialect varies in her poems. Keeping intact the philosophical content, I substitute archaic words with modern ones for easier comprehension, although I have to then alter the poem's meter.

Kabir:
Sufiana Ghazal

Why not listen to that ceaseless song which can be heard
Not only inside temples and mosques but outside as well?

Those of religious orders wear specific colours but if
They're not enlightened, do their robes signify much?

Priests consult scriptures so they can preach,
But is knowledge without wisdom of any use?

By pilgrimages to holy cities you
Untie the knots of deceit, pilgrim?

Tulsi of Hathras: Sufiana Ghazal

Clean up your heart to make room for your beloved,
Sweep aside all thoughts to make room for your love.

One heart has endless desires, insatiable greed,
Then where's the space to place your beloved?

Look at the goings-on within you that
Distract, disturb and disempower you.

Listen carefully to Tulsi's voice—
It reveals secrets to find oneself.

Tulsi of Hathras: Sufiana Ghazal

Look! Be dazzled by your inner beauty.
Look! Be watchful of all your thoughts.

You can discover the secret lying inside,
If only you draw aside the dark curtain.

Finding your beloved is easy Taqi, *
It's just the search that is difficult.

Without an enlightened guide,
No road can lead to salvation.

*Tulsi addresses his friend and fellow-seeker Sheikh Taqi.

The Future of Light Classical Music

Distanced in time from its courtesan background, Thumri's sensuality has been sanitized. Thumri's survival is ensured through Khayal singers, who usually conclude a concert with a *bhajan* or *thumri*. In presenting a *thumri* they mainly observe its Raga aspect, randomly wandering within a *raga*. Bol-banaana needs specific training.

Thumri's allied forms of Dadra, Kajri, Jhoola, Sawan, Hori and Chaiti may vanish along with traditional Thumri-oriented *ghazal-gayaki*. Wedged between classical and mainstream music—a space between "heavy" and "light" music—light classical music can thrive if nurtured, as it is finely balanced.

Classical and light classical genres are regarded as separate entities—which they are and yet are not—by music organizers or others who need neat labels, debarring light classical singers from participation in classical music festivals.

Artists need fame to showcase their talent. All brilliant singers are not famous and all famous singers are not brilliant. Begum Akhtar told me that some musicians get more fame than they deserve in any *zamana* (age) when a vacant area permits easy entry.

Western audiences can be receptive to this genre. The Smithsonian Institution in Washington DC—aware of *ghazal-gayaki*—lauded me as a "revivalist" for singing traditional Thumri-oriented Ghazal. After a concert in New York, I was surprised and pleased when an American told me "I know Begum Akhtar's music because I'm a huge fan and though it's obvious you've learnt from her, you've found your own sound". An Indian came backstage to thank me for introducing her to "a new kind of music" as she had never before heard Dadra, Hori, Jhoola or Kajri.